New Paths to Eden

New Paths to Eden

Poems by

Michael A. Griffith

© 2020 Michael A. Griffith. All rights reserved.
This material may not be reproduced in any form, published,
reprinted, recorded, performed, broadcast,
rewritten or redistributed without
the explicit permission of Michael A. Griffith.
All such actions are strictly prohibited by law.

Cover design by Shay Culligan

ISBN: 978-1-952326-29-5

Kelsay Books
502 South 1040 East, A-119
American Fork, Utah, 84003

This book is dedicated with much love and respect to every woman who helped shape my life and especially to Sharon Ramos McClellan. All paths have led to you.

Acknowledgments

Sincere thanks to the following sources for first publishing the poems listed below, some in different form:

Ariel Chart: "Comfort"
Communicator's League: "Vow"
Creative Talents Unleashed's anthology Microaggressions: "Acclimation"
Degenerate Literature: "1"
Foxglove Journal: "New Haven"
Impspired: "Bereft," "Love," "The Affair"
Indiana Voice Journal: "Mitosis" (as "Embers")
Persian Sugar in English Tea: A Bilingual Anthology of Short Poems and Haikus (Volume 1): "The Tall, Old Tree"
Poetry Quarterly: "Firefly"
Stanzaic Stylings: "Gently in Nature"
The Blue Nib: "Gem Show," "Remnants," "The Couple's Prayer"
The Disappointed Housewife: "Message"
The Drabble: "Steam"
The Lake: "Denim"
The Wild Word: "Beyond" (as "Not Meant to Be Liked")
Zombie Logic Review: "The Pines" (as "Dark")

Thank you to Emma Lee, Anne Walsh Donnelly, and Isabelle Kenyon for their helpful feedback on my manuscript for this book.

Contents

The Game	13
Wishes	15
Denim	16
Weave	17
The Tall, Old Tree	19
1	20
The Light of Her Heart	21
Gently in Nature	22
Comfort	23
Gem Show	24
Acclimation	25
Be My Yoko Ono	26
Bereft	27
The Couple's Prayer	28
Love	29
The Affair	31
Message	32
Steam	33
Beyond	34
Fallen	35
Vow	37
The Pines	38
Remnants	39
Strands	40
Mitosis	41
Firefly	42
New Haven	43

I meet you.
I remember you.
Who are you?
You destroy me.
You're so good for me.

How could I have known that you were made to the size of my body?

—Marguerite Duras, <u>Hiroshima Mon Amour</u>

The Game

Tracy and I in a north woods cabin
rented for the week by my dad and his best friend;
the smell of breakfast's bacon on the ground floor,
her mom's perfume upstairs.

She is 15, I am 13.
She is learning to smoke, and I watch.
One of her mom's Salems stolen from the nightstand,
a red Bic squeezed into her shorts pocket,
tanned legs draped over the bed.

Her spurts of coughs and laughter musical,
her eyes a green like my cat's.
Hot breezes slither through the open windows.
Our moms went into town shopping
 and our dads are out fishing.

The radio is on the only station other than gospel
or the Red Sox game I'd stayed to catch.
A song with French words, pulsations, and
gitchie-gitchie-ya-yas fights the static
and Tracy grabs my hand, jumps off the bed, swirling to dance.

I bob—legs piston as she spins and sings along,
hips pumping to the gitchie ya-yas in perfect time…
Perfect.

I stop to watch. Her eyes are closed,
in rapture. I am frozen,
devoted.
The cigarette pinched in her teeth,
that drop of sweat trailing down her neck…

Then the car's clatter coming into the shale driveway.
Radio off, cigarette tossed out the window.
I scram to my room
and our moms enter the cabin
calling out with groceries.

Tracy sprays more of the perfume, prances
downstairs to help.
I follow a minute later, the music,
the images still stuck in my mind.
Mom asks if I caught any of the game and I lie,
telling her I was reading instead.

There was never another time when Tracy and I were left alone
and that trip was the last time I'd ever see her.
My parents and hers didn't seem to talk all that much
after that summer. I asked Dad about this once
and I think he lied to me.

Wishes

Hot August night, 11th grade about to start. Thunder
wakes me just past four, and I am now too alert to sleep.

I listen to the storm, the rain striking the slate roof above me,
the box fan in my window whirring.

The sheets are damp from sweat.
I know somewhere people are making love right now.

It is not sex, not just biological; it is clean as rain.
I know that love follows the act as thunder follows the flash.

But I am filled with sex, filled with urge. The heat, my sweat,
the night, the storm, all bring thoughts and aching need.

I uncover and take care of biology.

The heat breaks. I roll over to watch the lightning, follow
the shadows' dance along the wall. Night moves to dawn as

the storm moves south. I go downstairs
and watch the first-shift traffic pass the house,

wonder if any of the drivers saw the storm, made love
in its sounds and light.

The street is wet, tires making slick sounds gliding on it.
Sounds like wishes, wishes clean, clean as love.

Denim

The most vibrant woman in my world
at that moment of her leaving—
Godiva's hair, St. Joan's confidence, the Mona Lisa's smile,
and her own unique laugh,
all in denim, with heavy backpack slung.

I would have gone over, stopped her,
made possessive love to her
had other faces not seen us,
other voices not owned us,
other hands not held ours.

She was saying some over-the-shoulder comment
I've since forgotten but would now pay blood to recall.
The moment's movement plays on,
loops, with only a din.
Her words are now gone.

They might have been nothing more than "late for class"
or they might reveal the reason
why she lives as she does now:
hair cut short, not so confident, a less-famous smile,
and a more common laugh.

Weave

                                          Too many stories,
                      two too many faces to you,
                             Chimera with a lilt.

                                Fickle, thin-skinned,
                 yet tough enough to laugh and
                                         to mean it.

                      Tough on those around you.
                          Rough around the edges.

I tell stories,
I show a face,
Minotaur with a maze to navigate.

Stubborn, thick-willed,
my laugh soon fades, but
I still mean it.

Tough to let others in.
Rough to be near.

                      We talk
               We joke
          We laugh
      We blush
           We hint
               We weave
  a dance of words,   this dance of
     intentions.

Our dance of glances

        not long held.

                If our eyes would stay, we would melt
                        some of your roughness,
                        some of my resolve.
                        So we look away.

                                        You move off with shifting faces,

I go back into my twisting ways.

The Tall, Old Tree

Meet me under the tall, old tree.
Beneath wide limbs so thick and full of leaves,
nobody will know, nobody will see.

We will embrace and I'll hold you
with arms full of strength and rustic longing
as I tell you things you want to be true.

We'll create our own heat and storm.
Sheltered there, no one will know what we do
in the tall tree. Lost in its huge, hard form,

close as vines entwined in the dark,
we will always be there if you believe
our two souls shall show as lines in tree bark.

Come meet me under that tall, old tree.
Nobody will know. Nobody will see.
Meet me there soon. Come closer. Be with me.

1

Logic counts in numbers
the heart cannot understand.
A math of mistakes and matches,
mayhem until numbers combine.

Add, subtract, multiply, divide.
(Don't forget to carry that "1.")

Fractions,
        oh damn...
                fractions.

Fractures of a family,
friendships add up to benefits:
perks, peeks, pets.
   (Sweat yet?)

                    Logic can go to Hell in its own tidy little
                            hand basket
since the heart wants what the heart wants when the heart wants
                                what does her heart want?

            (Why doesn't she call me?
        What, I'm not even worth a text?)

            Okay: Breathe + breathe =

            ...double-check the math...

        + (X-1) $\leq 3 \div$ $\neq 1$ ... = 2?

                    (Forgot to carry my one.)

The Light of Her Heart

Maiden fair swore her unending love
to knight gallant as she wrapped her lace
'round his shield arm and he bent to offer his long kiss.

Left he did to fates she could not fathom, and
as he made away, he could not see she
plucked her heart out from her slight chest.

Her mother gray, weeping, was not surprised to see it lit.
"Shield it, my girl, ere wind kill its flame." Maiden fair
looked away and whispered "Tears. Only tears will kill this."

Now at temple, that grave maiden places her heart
among those whose own knights have gone
and she tries not to cry onto their failing flames.

Gently in Nature

Today's sunlight will last forever in my memory.

Our sky a blue that can't be defined by a crayon's name.
Neither can the amber of your hair—
They're both found gently in nature.

We witness the park's afternoon together,
but details will shift in time's shaky embrace.

You will correct me when I misremember
the breed of the runaway dog we saw
and the name of that gas station where we bought
those regrettable stale sandwiches
when I tell our friends about this perfect picnic day.

But for now, all I want to focus on
is that spark in your smile as you look up
into my squinting-in-the-sun eyes,
the shine of love found gently in your nature.

Comfort

Our house is cold, and you are gone.
Cats curled into circles and even with the heat up,
the cold won't recede.

Taking down the Christmas cards,
sweeping the floor, other lonely tasks
take me back to this morning's first sight:

your legs exposed from beneath the thick comforter.
In the morning light, the gold of your skin,
the slow movement of flesh, the curve of your calves,

all formed a quiet sonata.
The performance becomes real only when
we are both awake and joined under the covers,

warm in embrace, warm in symphony—
harmony too soon interrupted
by tasks and duties.

Our house will soon be warm again,
filled with music all our own.
Tasks done, we become each other's comforter.

Gem Show

Tanzanite. Dinosaurs dancing as emojis try to talk.
Charity popcorn in five flavors. Autism speaking
as several cancers spread.

Aquamarine. I care about cancer more now that we are in love,
but I still don't fear my death. Just yours.

Amber. Fly with me. Be still with me. Get
stuck in me.

Diamond. Shine just for me. Dance only for me. Talk to me.

Jade. Be old with me.

Acclimation

Have I changed for you,
a better fit, a better fate?

Have you changed for me,
a bitter taste now an acquired one?

Do we absorb and expand
or retract and regroup?

Melting pot never quite hot enough,
nor stirred in the right ways for

all spices to become flavors.
Dance and swirl, centrifuge of life

a song we lonely sense, never really hear,
never quite get those words out right.

Mix, stir, many-to-one
yet alone at day's end

in skins our own unique shade.
Stripes, spots, splotches, clean as ivory and teeth

beautiful as any trophy and kept as pure
as our dance will allow.

Do I move to your rhythm
or do you come for my words?

Will I misshape you to my desire
or will you mold me to your will?

Be My Yoko Ono

Give me the reason to change who I think I am
and leave "yes" where I expect to see "no."

Let me become virginal once more.

Be a message I see in a cloud
and the reason for my divorce.

Be my heroin.

Come infuse my blood with need
and help break up my band.

Help me to look more like you.

Let me finish each of your sentences in public
and I'll let you have the last word at home.

Leave a bad taste in everyone's mouth but mine.

Be the meal the diner ran out of,
and the song whose lines I forget.

Be the mother of my next son.

Deny me, feed me, nurse me
and ground me once you've shown me

what truths heaven can hold.

Bereft

For Jen Orlick and Kathy Shimmel.

And as sunlight blushes our dawn
we hear fate spin its sleek loom—
clock ticks, clock ticks,
clock ticks, alarm.
Appointments, commitments, defeats.
Each day eats the other, eats the other,
eats the next, bleed.
Days bleed as need begets need.
Energy needs matter to matter.
Form become force as one
becomes all.
Becomes all for one.
One bleeds, all bleed.
Bleeding begets blood begets love
begets force begets energy begets
theft. Envy. Memory/Desire to be one,
to behold, to be held, to be.

Be as you are in my dawn, be.
Brush my cheek softly.
Turn off the clock.
Burn the calendar.
Beget time.
Just for me.

The Couple's Prayer

Thy will be done
as our kingdom comes.

Forgive me as I forgive you
as you trespass against me.

I hallow your name as you
deliver me from evil
and give me a day's bread.

Led into temptation, forgive me,
for I am bound to your heaven.

In all your power,
in all your glory,
now and forever,
thy will be done.

Love

How can I help you? the home robot asks
as I tap the screen for my morning game.

She gives me the same dopamine rush,
just with different apps.
Different apps by day, different apps by night.

How can I help you?

I'm hungry.

I curse the old toaster for burning my bread
as the 'fridge tells me that I'm low on eggs
and high in cholesterol.

The robot discards the burnt toast and toaster.
The drone will have new here by lunch.

How can I help you?

Endless choices, all familiar, from
age-appropriate algorithms,
records of in-game choices, viewing preferences,
prior purchases, and R&D.

How can I help you?

I open the front door to smell the breeze
as my doorknob tells me the weather:
Chilly, a bit damp; a soft rain later today.

The coatrack turns, offering me the right hat,
the best coat for the weather.

I command it to stop.
I want to feel the chill, the breeze.

How can I help you?

The rack keeps spinning, pushing the hat and coat my way.

I repeat the command.

How can I help you?

I close the door.

How can I help you?

The rack keeps spinning.

How can I help you?

There is no breeze to smell.

The Affair

I pass the salt and glance up as she attracts my attention:
the woman in the window,
three stories up and naked.

Our eyes meet across Second Avenue and I am frozen at my table.

She wraps herself in the sheer drapes
then peels some away, their satiny shine playing
against her coffee-with-cream skin.
Gliding her hand down her throat she smiles, showing
the tips of her teeth.

My wife says something as our waiter draws near.
The draped woman turns as if interrupted,
intruded-upon, then departs.

Only the drapes' swirl and my spilled water betray our deed.

Message

MAILER DAEMON dead letter
regret if never sent re: gret
if said too much to much too little
grow
as narcissi blind
echo deaf
centrifugation of tongue
calibration of tone
concertation of two
   1
win

come twin come
seek
the conjoinal scars
weshare

Steam

Another man's woman is making me breakfast.
She says it's the reverse-supper she needs to make
for her night-shift husband anyway.

She's telling me something else, some story
I'm meant to follow, but I'm not really listening.

I needed last night as much as she did.
I don't feel sorry or wrong, exactly. I feel
empty.

Steam rises from the pan next to her. She turns to stir the eggs and
I wish I'd left ten minutes ago.

Coffee?
No,
thank you.

Beyond

I never knew what a drug felt like until I met you.
Never knew a fever was not meant to be feared.
Never knew that thirst was a good thing.
Never knew crazy, never knew ill,
never knew such a love was not meant to be liked.

And we loved it all
until the drug ran out,
until the fever burned us to blisters and ash,
until the thirst drove us in two different ways
and our illness spread
beyond
us.

Fallen

Whose arms, woman, whose arms, girl?
Whose arms were strongest as they held you?

Daddy's as you grew bigger then pulled away and ran
or that pushy first boy's who thought he was an anaconda
but was really just a snake?

Husband, maybe?
Didn't he feel like Superman when
                              you

                        fell

                        for

                            him?

Lover-boy other toy, pastor, shrink,
pool boy, UPS man, man down the Jiffy Lube,
man in the moon?

Does even he have arms long and strong enough
to reach down, to hold you,
then lift you up, up and away?

To swaddle you, embrace you, to protect you?

Where do you want your man,
on top, on bottom, on his knees, on all fours?

Bark, dog, bark!
Slither, snake, slither...

Don't give trust too quickly, girl;
don't alms away your love so fast, woman.

Eve's serpent had a man's voice, after all,
and one bite is as sinful as the next.

Vow

Lipstick stains my wineglass.

I loved her long before the grapes
were harvested,
turned to a red deeper than her stain,
less intoxicating than her lips.

Stick to stone, break the bone—
broken words can always hurt me.

Vow   do us   part.

Death may still kiss my bride,
a willful bride to a willing death.

She: Look how lovely in white!
He: How handsome in his best suit,
gray as smoke-layer atop a pyre.

The Pines

Them dark pines out back, as tall as they are dark.
They hide what don't need showin';
dark at noon, dark like midnight.

They hide a bit of me
an' a good bit of you.
They hide what I don't want known.

There among them tall, dark pines,
bones green with moss an' leaf-fall.
They lay there, hid, overgrown roots
tangled 'round bones half-buried.

Them pines sway only on dark winds,
like that sawblade time they was blowin'
when you tried to leave me an' go to him.

Dark words met dark minds
met dark hearts met dark blood
met dark dirt.

Three years gone now.
The pines feed on your dark
an' they feed on my dark.

Three dark anniversaries gone.
Your bones cold there, hid,
but I can still feel our hot old sins
when them pines get to whisperin' with the wind.

Remnants

After Rebecca Askew

There are things meant to remain behind:

Odd socks, mismatched gloves, my good
shirt you stained with cooking oil

That gold ring never worn again,
though to once have taken it off would have
seemed a sin

Notes, lists, movie ticket stubs, fortunes
from cracked cookies, tucked
inside and between shelved books

Photos too much parts of ourselves to be
thought of as garbage or to be seen
by the eyes of another

That roadmap for the trip south
we never had time to take

Songs, night music from drives and bedrooms
we sometimes listen to, to cry

Marks where you left them, accidentally or not

A voice I hear in the late night and a name I use
at the wrong time

The ache

Strands

Why deny the obvious necessity for memory?
—Marguerite Duras, Hiroshima Mon Amour

Walked through her spider's web
on my way to take in the sun.

The silkhair strands stick to my skin,
eerie tracings of where her fingers
once slid.

As the sun bakes my flesh.
I feel the strands melting into me,
phantom limbs of amputated desire.

I should move to the healing shade.
(That coolness beckons.)

But baking, simmering in her strands seems
somehow more enticing, more satisfying,
than that soothing shade
I see
inching away.

Mitosis

When nuclear war was the realists' fear,
before AIDS, Ebola, Ebonics, eBay—
we split, divided before these things evolved.

Live Aid was our Woodstock,
nouveau hippies, pseudo cools,
so in love on smoke-hazed weekends.

Your cells traveled so far, while mine
stayed, comfortable in the petri dish gel
as we both expanded apart.

I wish we could join together,
form a temporary tissue,
relive our past as cameras can,

if even just for some hours
to feel the haze once more,
smoke leading to fire to see ourselves

once more as we were,
with membranes of what we've become
not mutations of what we might have been.

Firefly

I could have caught you as a boy
but never would as a man.
You flit, you flutter, you shine then go dark.

Your dancing and movements so fast
I could only hope but fall and be lost
in a cloud of your dust.

There are sides of you only I saw
but still so many left unseen—
wings and dance, a flight unique.

What you showed me was enough to
give me pause, to thrill me, entice me,
to stay with me all these years of nights later.

I know you fly best by night,
shine best, too; paint the sky
in the trail of your own fire.

Fly, then, flutter and flit.
Fit where you find yourself,
and find that you fit there well.

New Haven

I miss the flowers of our old garden—
roses, foxglove, bleeding hearts, lilacs, and lilies.

We had a garden that,
when tended well,
looked like a part of Eden.

You have a new "our;"
I have a new "we."

Both will start new gardens,
plant familiar flowers.
But enough new will grow
to make new paths to Eden.

Same sun, different rays, different light.
Different rainbows from opposite arcs.
Stars set differently in the same sky;
yours night while I see day.

Our own clouds upon which to build new castles,
each its own new haven for two.

About the Author

Michael A. Griffith is the author of the chapbooks *Bloodline* (The Blue Nib) and *Exposed* (Soma Publishing). He began writing poetry while recovering from a disability-causing injury. Mike lives in central New Jersey and teaches at Raritan Valley Community College.

https://twitter.com/AuthorMGriffith

https://michaelgriffithwordpress.wordpress.com

www.ingramcontent.com/pod-product-compliance
Lightning Source LLC
Chambersburg PA
CBHW022001100426
42738CB00042B/1329